CHADBURY

A TOWN AND INDUSTRIAL SCAPE IN 'O' GAUGE

CHADBURY

A TOWN AND INDUSTRIAL SCAPE IN 'O' GAUGE

Eric Bottomley GRA

PEN & SWORD
TRANSPORT

First published in Great Britain in 2017 by
Pen & Sword Transport
An imprint of Pen & Sword Books Ltd
47 Church Street
Barnsley
South Yorkshire
S70 2AS

ISBN 9781473876323

Typeset by Milepost 92½
Printed and bound by Replika Press Pvt. Ltd

Typeset in Palatino

Pen & Sword Books Ltd incorporates the imprints of Pen & Sword
Archaeology, Atlas, Aviation, Battleground, Discovery, Family History,
History, Maritime, Military, Naval, Politics, Railways, Select, Social
History, Transport, True Crime, and Claymore Press, Frontline Books,
Leo Cooper, Praetorian Press, Remember When, Seaforth Publishing
and Wharncliffe.

For a complete list of Pen and Sword titles please contact
Pen and Sword Books Limited
47 Church Street, Barnsley, South Yorkshire, S70 2AS, England
E-mail: enquiries@pen-and-sword.co.uk
Website: www.pen-and-sword.co.uk

DEDICATION

A complete model railway encompasses many skills and I certainly do not have all of them. Therefore I would like to dedicate this book to three people who have helped me over the years to create 'Chadbury'. Alphabetically they are 'Adge' Henshaw, Norton Jensen, and Fred Lewis. I thank them for their skills their time and their friendship. May our teapot never go cold !

E.B.

I would also like to thank the following for their invaluable help - to my dear wife Jacqui for her help and 'understanding' also Paul Beatty, Philip D Hawkins, David Mocatta, & John Scott-Morgan.

Photography by James Purssell
Track plan CAD Keith Wesley

CONTENTS

INTRODUCTION

My career in illustrating transport scenes and especially railways inevitably led me to the world of model railways. Initially through a meeting with Peter Farish, the then managing director of Grafar model railways, who commissioned me to paint a picture of a 'Black 5' to co-inside with their latest model of this loco in 'N' gauge (2mm- foot). In the 1970's 'N' gauge was gaining popularity at this time as it suited small rooms, even a table top could support a reasonable model railway layout. Later Grafar commissioned me to produce a series of model buildings. After photographing the type of buildings we had discussed I then set about drawing them to scale twice the size they were to be printed. They were printed on sticky backed paper to be cut out and stuck on to a series of blocks provided. Everything from terraced houses to factories and of course railway stations, bridges, goods warehouses etc.

It was great fun choosing various buildings around the Poole and Wimborne area where I lived at that time. It also gave me a greater awareness of design and proportion, useful many years later when building my 'O' gauge layout Chadbury. On my trips back home to my parents in Lancashire I would photograph some remaining industrial buildings, such as cotton mills and factories that were being demolished or adapted for other usage. I often wondered what passing motorists thought of this odd person with his tape measure across a cotton mill window!

In Peter Farish's effort to help me to get on in my career he introduced me to model railway exhibitions by allotting me space to exhibit my paintings on the Grafar trade stand. I remember being awestruck at the size of the International Model Railway Exhibition (IMREX) at Wembley conference centre. I marvelled at the model railway layouts and my involvement with 'N' gauge soon leaped across 'OO' to a greater interest in 'O' gauge. My first 'purchase' being a barter for one of my paintings in return for an industrial Pecket 0-6-0 saddletank. This in turn led me to purchase the Sevenscal kit for a Lancashire & Yorkshire 0-4-0 Pug. I seem to remember the wording on the instructions saying 'can be built with a few simple tools'. I soon realised my limitations as a kit builder having put together body and cab; then to the rescue came a kit building friend who fitted the motor and gearbox and told me that my 'few simple tools' were not up to the job. Since then I have left loco kit building to persons more suited to that purpose, with skill and patience that eludes me in that direction.

Graham Farish's Scenecraft building kits have revolutionised scenery construction for the railway modeller. Unlike expensive factory-built models or flimsy, cardboard cutouts which can prove difficult to assemble, Scenecraft buildings use plastic blocks and printed adhesive facades to create a highly realistic and inexpensive addition to your layout which even children will enjoy making.

Grafar buildings continued:

8F No. 48523 and WD No. 90257 double-head a coal train past the canal basin.

Looking down Bridgewater Street.

My first wharf building straddling the canal with Peckett 0-4-0 industrial saddletank busy at work.

CHADBURY

So I had to build my own layout, but what would it represent? Well, without any hesitation it had to depict the Lancashire townscape in which I grew up, with cotton mills, factories and endless rows of terraced houses. Not only did this represent my boyhood surroundings but the buildings themselves would offer me great scope in modelling.

This photo depicts a time when cotton was king and a working man's life meant nothing but toil and poverty. Rows of terraced houses sat in the shadows of dark satanic mills. My home town of Oldham was such a place. By 1921 it had built 320 cotton mills and at that time was employing 34,264 people. Much of this industrial architecture still remained during my childhood leaving indelible memories in me and provided the inspiration for Chadbury.

In total contrast to the above at the time my layout began I was living in the rural county of Herefordshire in an Old Coach House in the lovely village of Much Marcle near Ledbury. It had an enormous garage which in days past was owned by the Vicar and housed his coach and horses with stables at the rear. This vacuous space was wasted so I had

a floor put in to create two upstairs rooms and knocked a doorway through to the house. I needed the space to house my ever growing stock of fine art prints and greeting cards, so above all this I would create the 'O' gauge layout. The baseboards were in fact the melamine doors that I had replaced throughout the house with pine doors. I had a whole stack of them and in this day and age of recycling it seemed a great shame to waste them. These doors of course had their faults for when it came to wiring the track we had to get the wires through two layers of plywood with a cardboard filled vacuum inside. The good thing about them was they were light and ideal for canal modelling as you could cut through the top ply and scrape out the cardboard making a perfect depth for canal use. I fixed a batten all round the walls of the two rooms and sat the doors on this, then attached legs to the front screwed into the floor. The baseboards now in position it was down to track work. The track I bought was Peco streamline fine standard bullhead rail. The name 'Chadbury' is derived from the first part of Chadderton (Oldham) where I grew up, and Bury where my wife Jacqui comes from.

My old playground, the Rochdale Canal, Chadderton , Oldham 1970s

TRACK PLAN

Although Chadbury is a layout that began in Herefordshire in 2000, it had to be transported down to Devon in 2012 to a different shape and format. The Old Coach House layout was 4.57m x 8.53m (15ft x 28ft) in size using two upstairs rooms with holes cut through the walls either side to allow the track to pass through. Typical of roof space layout, it had sloping ceilings on three sides only allowing me one gable end wall to accommodate my large buildings.

The current layout, now in Devon, is housed in a 5.18m (17ft) square double garage integral to the house. 39sq metres (420 sq. ft) down to 26.8 sq metres (289 sq. ft) meant a totally different layout. Visitors staying in the bedroom adjacent to the double garage are now blessed with an en-suite model railway!! The plus side of the new venue are four walls eight feet high for me to cover with a painted sky in oils using 3" brushes followed by a watercolour painted backdrop which takes the eye gradually from the modelled buildings of three dimensions to the painted backdrop of two dimensions.

Starting with the empty garage space, with the help of a builder, we had to seal the large garage door shut and take out all the automatic door mechanism. Giving me a clean space to start with. The builder fixed battens down the walls at 40cm apart then screwed 2.43m x 1.21m (8ft x 4ft) sheets of hardboard all round. We eliminated the hard corners by bending the hardboard to form a smooth continual surface for me to paint. I then had the task of refitting the base boards 'doors' to the new shape. The ceiling was covered in sheets of foam insulation board to give me an even flat surface on which to paint a grey neutral sky. This was done with black and white emulsion paints mixed to a medium grey. This colour also for the tops of the base boards and the corked areas on which the track would be laid. To give me maximum space for the track I created a tunnel on which I stood my large buildings. Anyone who models in 'O Gauge' will appreciate how quickly it eats up space on your layout.

The green area denotes all the elevated part of the layout including the 'cotton mill line' and the 'timber line' from G. Hancock's building. The pink area denotes Bridgewater Street, not physically attached to the layout enabling me to pull it away in order to tend to the layout behind.

The track layout started with two maximum size circles leaving just enough width for building facades sat on retaining walls to have lighting inside. The four corners allowing me much more scope for modelling larger buildings with more depth. The elevated section on the north wall opposite the doorway has the Cliff Mill, the C.W.S. Factory and L & Y Rly. goods warehouse above the tunnel section.An elevated line known as the cotton mill line runs across the front of these buildings with an industrial saddle tank and a few wagons in operation. The left hand west wall has a track point off the inside main line to allow locos into the shed area and a somewhat convoluted run to the water and coal stage. Opposite this the east wall has the station area and a run through to a head shunt and single track goods platform. A point from the inside main line into the station is just on the right beyond the girder bridge. To the left of the door is an independent short track by the canal. Finally the elevated track known as the timber line runs from G Hancock & Sons Timberworks across a metal viaduct and down the east wall to disappear behind the town centre buildings. Due to the very sharp curves this can only be operated by an O-4-O ST, ex L & Y Pug with a few wagons. Both the independent lines are operated by an auto reverse timer system not connected to the main and DCC running.

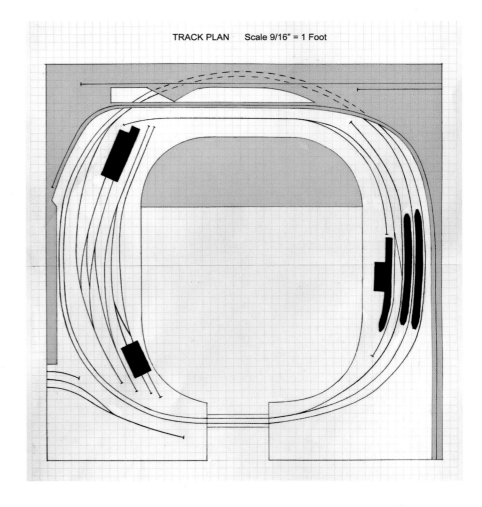

TRACK PLAN   Scale 9/16" = 1 Foot

MAKING
A FACTORY
BUILDING
(NORTON R. JENSEN IRONWORKER)

This is a versatile industrial building suited to virtually anywhere on this layout. I have situated it beside a canal as it could act as an early Victorian factory dependant on the waterway network for transportation. After manufacturing had ceased as many of these buildings had after the war, they were just used for the storage of goods to be moved either by road or by rail.

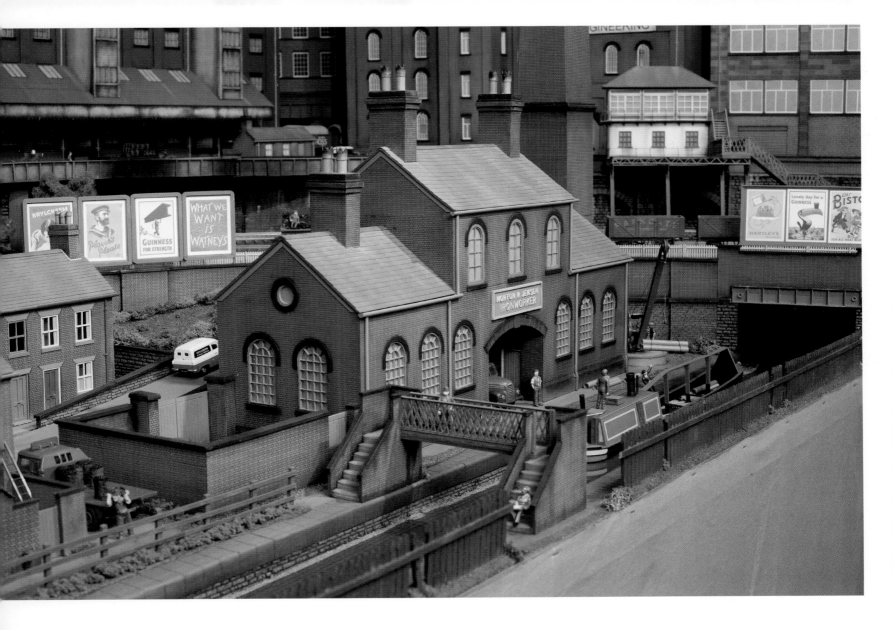

Loading metal tubes (in actual fact, paintbrush bristle protectors) to a narrow boat by Norton R Jensen's ironworks.

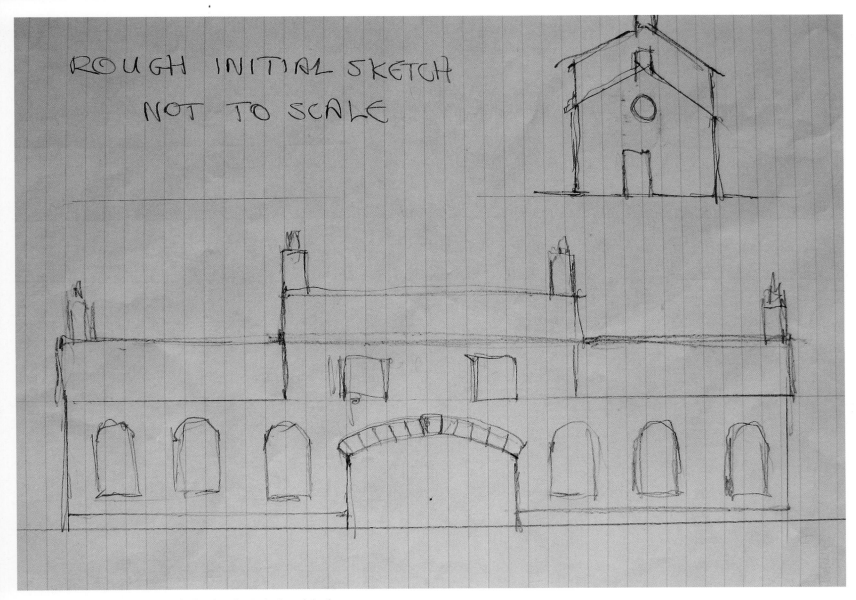

ROUGH INITIAL SKETCH
NOT TO SCALE

1. I have started with a rough sketch. A basic design of the factory.

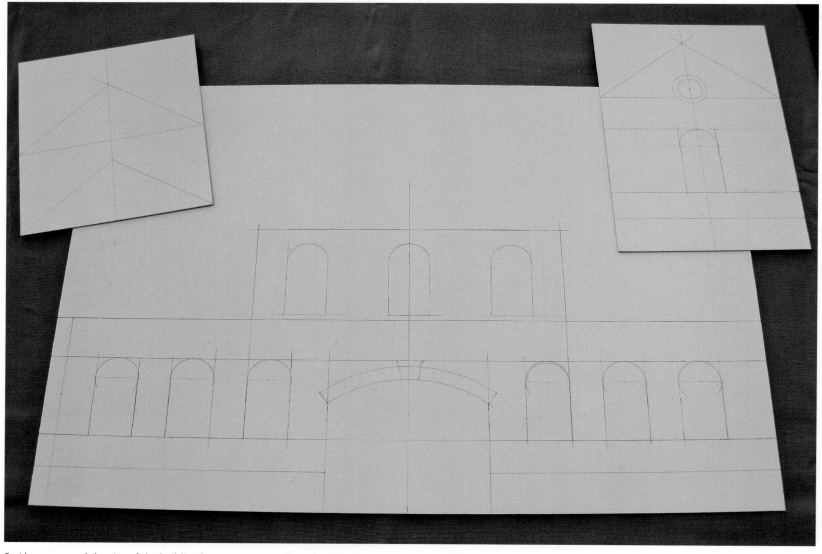

2. I have guessed the size of the building by spacing out six white metal moulded windows either side of an archway. Sat above the arch could be offices, this time using plastic moulded windows.

3. With Stanley knife and steel rule I've cut out the shape of the building made from mount board. Here I have taken extra care cutting the curved tops so the moulded windows fit snugly into the aperture. Front and back of the building are identical with the archway running through. One of the two ends has two more white metal windows, the other will have a tall factory chimney and door attached.

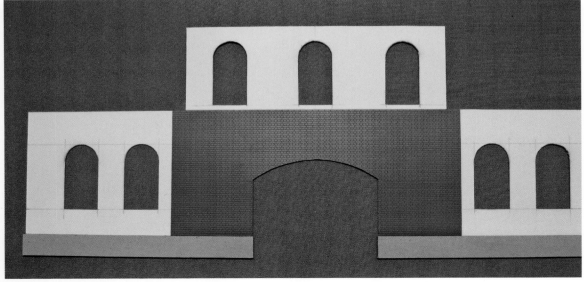

4. I have stuck extra strips of card along the base of the walls to represent stonework jutting out. This also gives the building more strength.

5. I then stick on my brick plasticard making sure that where two sheets meet is at a point where I can disguise the join with a drainpipe. I cut the plasticard to the shape of the building so as not to waste any surplus. I spread impact adhesive to both surfaces very thinly then put them together right away, making sure I place them exactly where I want, as this glue does not give you any time for movement. Using a piece of thick card or the end of a plastic ruler pressing the plasticard down.

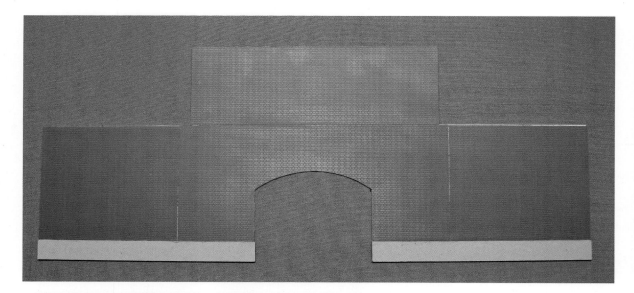

6. Turning the wall round I then cut out the plasticard round the window apertures from the back with a scalpel or craft knife, cleaning the edge after with medium grade sandpaper. (Note: when gluing with impact adhesive I take care not to get it on the front of the model and I wipe any surplus off with white spirit as soon as possible.)

7. For the eyebrows above the windows I used a compass with pencil to draw eight circles to the window width. Then adding another 5mm (3/16th in.) drawing an outer circle. Drawing across the centres, halving the circle I then cut out with a scalpel the eyebrow to be stuck over the window. I have used very thin card for this so it appears to be flush with the brickwork. Saving the fiddly job of cutting out the plasticard brickwork to the eyebrow shape.

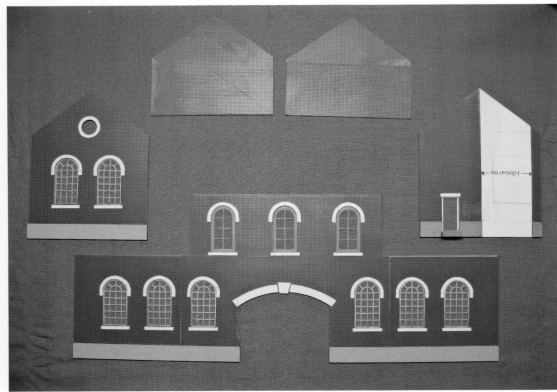

8. When window eyebrows, sills and the archway stonework have been stuck on, the next process is strengthening the edges of the building with pieces of strip wood 12mm (½ in.) square. Also used for PVA glueing the walls together.

9. Before this I 'weather' the wall sections (See page on 'weathering'). When the oil paint is dry, I stick plastic film behind the windows to glaze them and then tracing paper behind the film to fog the window. Windows can be painted either before or after weathering.

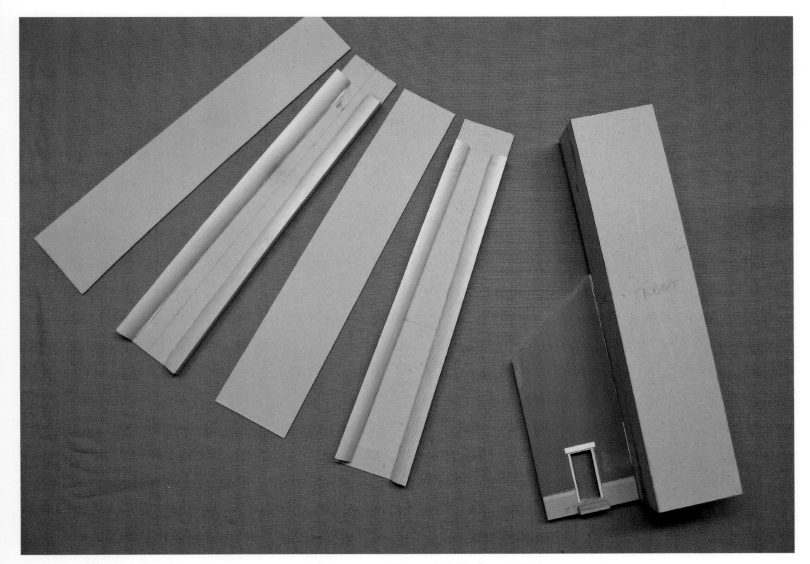

10. The main factory chimney is basically two sections made from 2mm MDF for strength. The lower half being square and parallel up to the height of the roof chimneys. A block of wood is glued in the top with a central piece jutting up for the top half to sit on. The top section is tapered with strips of card glued on the top to show the corbelling out of the brickwork. Thin strips of card are then stuck round the top part of the chimney to represent metal strapping.

11. I am now ready to assemble the walls, six in total including the two elevated walls for the offices above the archway. Using PVA I glue one end at a time and hold the sections with spring clips, checking with a set square that my walls are square. Also very useful for squaring is my 'Edding CM45 art mat' covered in grid squares to sit my building on.

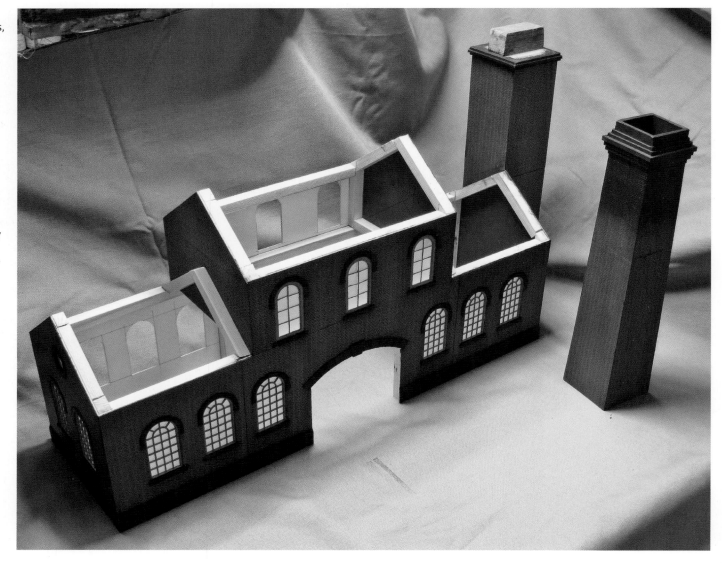

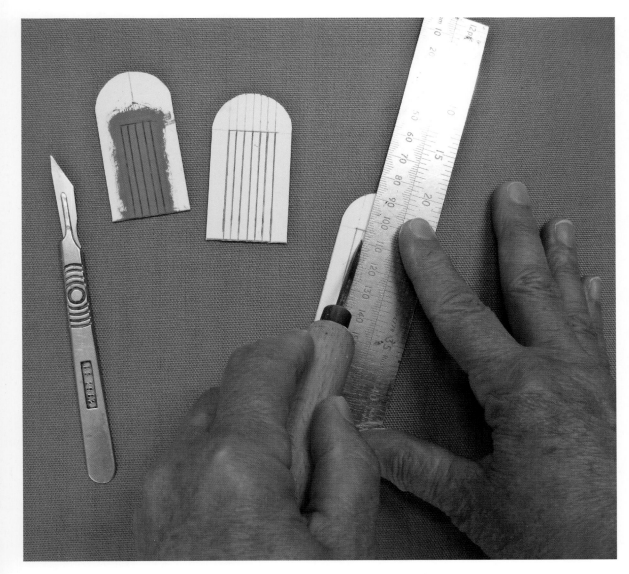

12. When making doors (or anything that is wooden boarded e.g. station canopies), after drawing out the correct shape and measuring the boards, in this case 3mm (1/8th in.) wide, I score down the pencil lines with craft knife and steel rule then swap knife for bradall and score down again pressing in the 'tongue and groove' effect. In this case I have used the mount board apertures cut from the windows. Mountboard has a good surface for cutting cleanly. There are three doors to make, one on the right side of the building adjacent to the large chimney and one either side of the centre passageway for entry to the factory left and right.

I have no fixed rule as to when I weather the buildings, but on this occasion I am 'weathering' the walls before I glue them together. The chimney of course will be solid black at the top with the paint gradually wiped off to the required effect.Apart from the main body of the factory are additional pieces to be measured, cut and painted. Plastic guttering, down pipes and three chimneys for the roofs.

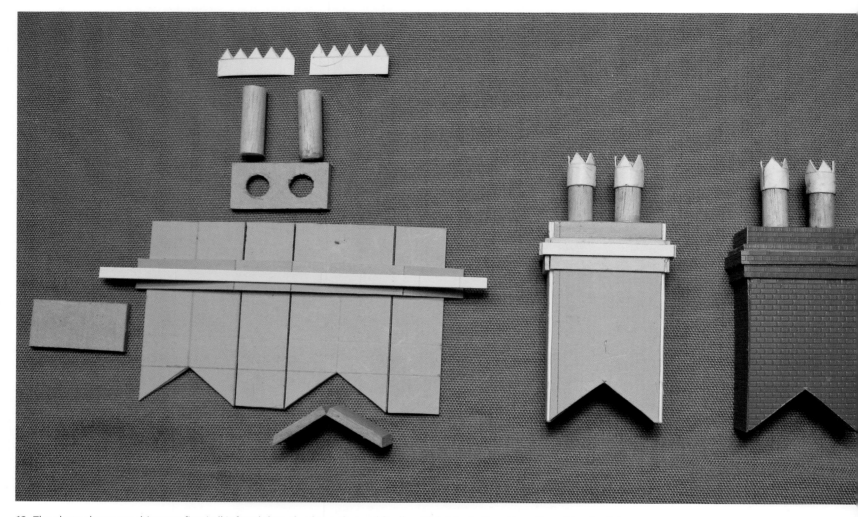

13. The photo shows my chimneys first in 'kit form' then glued together and finally with brick plasticard 'weathered' in oil paint. The chimney pots being dowel with thin card cut out to a crown shape. Before I attach my three roofs I stick a 50.8cm (20in.) length of wood through the centre of the building for the attachment of lighting in the form of LED's at a later date.

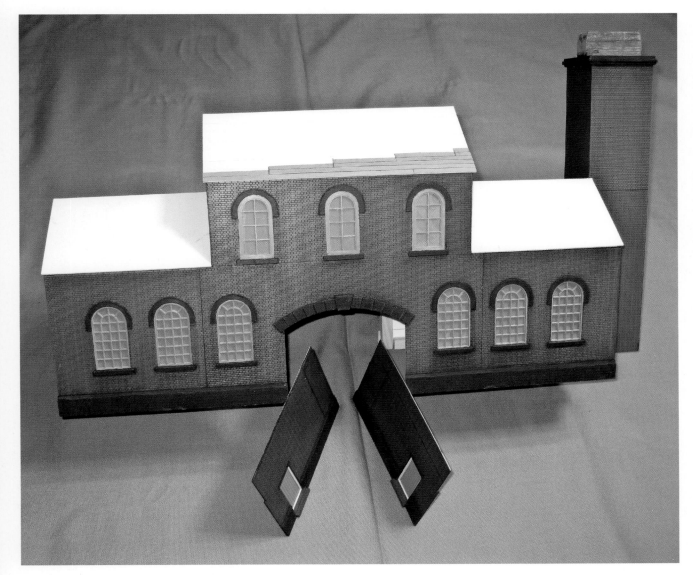

14. I have cut the roof pieces and stuck them on with PVA glue sticking on my three chimneys prior to tiling. For this I use strips of thin card 25mm (1in.) deep marked with a line half way along the strips for the overlapping tile effect. This also adds to the strength of the roof. Painting the roof I use the blue and brown oil colour mix but with more white to make a mid grey. The two inner passageway walls are added next. Tipping the factory on its back I then glue on the gutters and down pipes in their strategic places. Lastly I add the metal straps around the top half of the main chimney using thin plastic strip painted black.

15. This building I have dedicated to my good friend Norton Jensen, who over the years has taught and encouraged me through the hobby of model railways. The name board has plastic letters stuck on mountboard and painted in a weathered style. The whole building is 63.5cm (25in.) wide x 30.5cm (12in.) high. Chimney height 67.3cm (26.5in.)

MAKING TERRACED HOUSES

My rows of terraced houses are in fact 'three up two down', making them more effective when lit. In total I have made three blocks of four and two blocks of two with ginnels between. A pair of houses would share an outbuilding and small yard at the rear.

In situ complete with washing lines backing onto the canal.

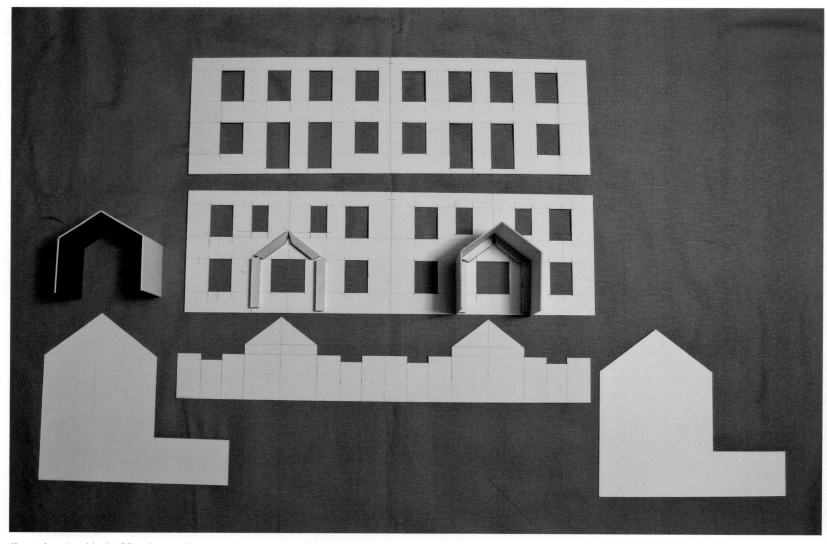

Shown here is a block of four houses drawn and cut out. Overall length being 40.6cm (16in.) The height to gutter is 127mm (5in.) and 171mm (6.75in.) to roof top. The depth of the house is 114mm (4.5in.)

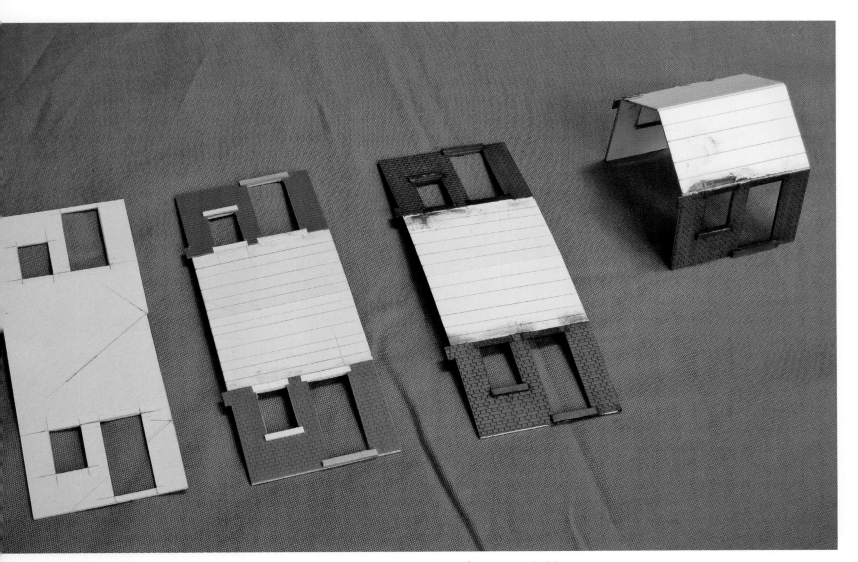

The photos will show two sets of four being made (as the demand for housing increases!) The rear outbuilding
I have cut in one piece and stuck the plastikard on while flat before attaching it to the house.

Other pieces in preparation are the door and window apertures to be attached behind the brick wall, and thin plastic strips for the window bars. Not shown here but also required would be lengths of guttering, drain pipes and rear gates.

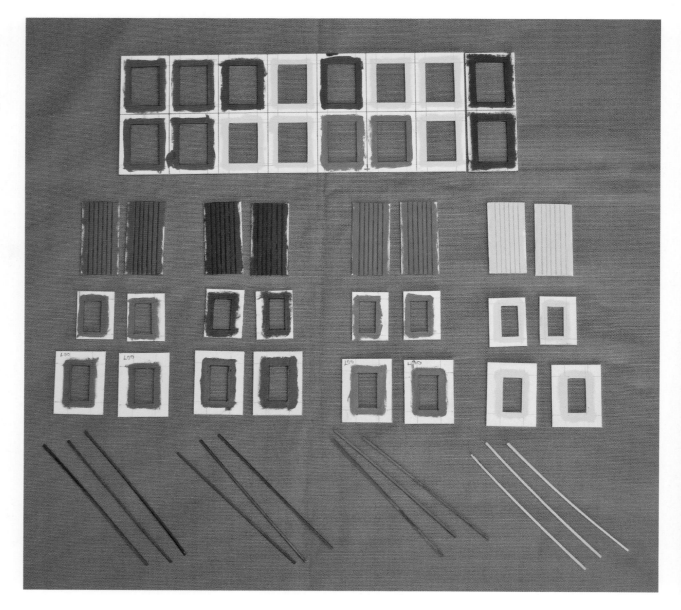

Glued to the rear wall are pieces of stripwood forming the shape of the outbuilding with a hole cut in the centre to allow the lighting to show through after the outbuilding has been attached. It is also easier to attach plasticard and small window and door to outbuilding while it is flat before gluing it to the wall.

Plasticard can be glued on before or after the outbuilding is attached.
Then the window apertures can be cut out from the inside.

Stripwood is then glued to the insides of the wall sections for assembly after the window apertures and doors are fixed in.
At this stage I have also weathered the sections prior to assembly while they can be laid flat (see page on weathering).

Having fixed the four walls and outbuildings I now attach the rear yard wall including the outbuilding gable end.
A short wall turned in at the corner and rear gate will be added next.

The main roof is now glued on. Once again one piece of mount board scored down the middle and bent over the gables makes for a much stronger structure. Chimneys are also ready to be glued on.

For roof tiling as per "Making a factory building"point 14,. strips of card 25mm (1in.) deep with a line drawn along halfway for the overlap. Make sure the first row of 'tiles' sits over the guttering to start with.

For card and wood I have used PVA white glue. For plastic products I use EVO-STIK impact adhesive. When gluing down pipes and guttering it is better to tip the building on its back in order to lay them on a flat surface.

CLIFF MILL

The first building I made was the 'Cliff' cotton mill. I named it after my father who was a bricklayer; and after the second world war, part of his work entailed repairing mills. He also worked on a new canteen building at Horwich railway works. Sadly he died in September 2000 and never saw my building finished. The mill has 166 windows all cut with scalpel and steel rule out of mountboard or thick card. Once I had measured the height and width of one window and the space between the next it was just a matter of repetition. The main body of the mill was cut out of 2mm MDF with a stanley knife and a steel rule. This was hard work but necessary due to the size of the building to give it strength. The window frames are stuck on the back of the window appatures with PVA glue then after that, plastic film, shiny on the window side, defused on the reverse is glued to the back of the window. Clear plastic film requires tracing paper to the back to defuse it in order to hide what lies behind. In the case of the Cliff mill I have a four foot flourescent tube fixed to the wall. I then cut thin strips of card to the required length and carefully, with tweezers, dip them in impact adhesive for a quicker drying time and placed them carefully on the pencil lines I had drawn for the window divisions. Some cotton mills were decorated with strips of cream coloured bricks travelling the full length of the building either above or below the windows. This colour can be achieved using a mix of yellow ochre and white and painted very carefully over the red plasticard brick. When totally dry this can be weathered very lightly to tone down the cream. The same colour (or white) can be used for the window frames and doors.

The Cliff mill is an amalgam of various mills made to my own design. The fun of model making is creating your own building based on the real thing. The top of the mill tower is embellished with four shampoo bottle tops, one at each corner, and in the centre four pieces of thin card tapered to represent the sheet lead tower top.

The overall size of the mill is 2.13m (7ft)wide including the tower and the offices to the left whose ten narrow vertical windows contrast nicely with the regular shaped windows of the mill itself. The main body of the mill is 55.9cm (22in.) high with the tower top being 101.6cm (40in.) high.

Ex LMS 8F waits to leave with a freight from Station Road goods.

As Hudswell Clark 0-4-0 saddletank approaches the cotton mill with four vans, the Jinty waits below with a similar goods train.

C.W.S

The C.W.S. (Co-operative Wholesale Society) buildings were a common sight up and down the country. The Co-op Store as I knew it in the 1950's and 60's was, I suppose, the forerunner of the modern day supermarket where people paid with 'real' money! And, as account holders were rewarded every so often with a dividend or 'divvy' as it was affectionately known. Children told to go to the shop would have to remember their 'divvy' number. Along with many cotton mills there was a C.W.S. Works which backed onto our railway line and during our train spotting, me and my pals would play amongst the hundreds of barrels in the C.W.S. yard outside the factory. The model is again ficticious but typical of the period. 94cm (37in.) high x 104cm (41in.) wide.

THE LANCASHIRE & YORKSHIRE RAILWAY
COMPANY GOODS WAREHOUSE

Once again, maximising on the gable wall in my previous house I made the L & Y Railway warehouse as big as possible. The overall size is 119cm (47in.) wide x 61cm (24in.) high to rooftop and 20.3cm (8in.) deep as a half building, the other half I painted on the backdrop to give the impression of a complete building. Typical of L & Y warehouses I based it on the one at Royton near Oldham. Towards the end, these buildings lost their shutes and canopies as the woodwork rotted and their use diminished. I carefully drew the lettering out on paper making sure that it fitted the respective gaps, then traced it down using white chalk on the reverse as pencil would not show up on the plasticard. Using my art school lettering skills I drew the letters by hand, but nowadays you could print them out from a computer and trace over.

Ex L&Y Pug No.51218 on the elevated timber line.

LANCASHIRE
AND YORKSHIRE
LWAY CO. GOODS
BRYLCREEM
WHAT WE
WANT

HOWELLS ENGINEERING

Named after my brother in law Dave Howell who was an engineer. This was the last of the tall buildings in my previous house, so tall it went up inside a velux window! With the windows shut of course! Like most of my buildings it was to my own design but typical of Victorian and Edwardian industrial architecture.

The metal moulded windows I bought in packs. I could not cut anything this fine by hand. The main building is made in two sections screwed together in the back. The right hand section under the sloping roof once again is only a half building, saving valuable space on the layout. The walkway bridge is made from mount board with a much thinner card curved over for the roof. An upside down birthday cake candle holder sits proudly atop of the tower 96.5cm (38in.) high.

Night time goods workings on both elevated lines.

McKENNA'S GLASS

M y other brother-in-law, Declan Mckenna, comes from Waterford in Southern Ireland so I named the building after him due to the connection with Waterford Crystal.

This is a more modern building maximising on the windows. Using mount board I drew out a rough pattern of stonework, and then with oil paint created a dirty stone effect. The lettering on top I drew out onto card, then cut out the letters with a craft knife, sticking them onto plastic strips. Declan's building stands 68.5cm (27in.) wide x 48.2cm (19in.) high.

G. HANCOCK & SONS TIMBER MERCHANTS

My good friend George Hancock has three sons, so George, working in the building industry, I thought, warranted the timber company. This houses quite a collection of lollypop sticks and other waste strips of wood stuck together with PVA glue. A good deal of imagination is required for the building's depth. I just thought the angle of the buildings made a change from the 'flat to the wall' facades of the other buildings.

This building had to be built twice almost as it was ruined by a leak from the flat roof above which ran down the wall at this point and loosened all the PVA glue inside. The leak also ran through my painted backdrop (painted in watercolour) and had to be re-painted all over again.

As a timber train enters the yard a 'Jubilee' on an express passes below.

HENSHAW ELECTRICAL

One of my longest standing friends, Adge Henshaw, has worked with electronics many years and has done a wonderful job wiring the layout track work and lighting all the buildings. Not surprising then he should have his own company to mark his achievements. When this layout came down to Devon I had the space to extend this building by raising it up another storey and adding two side pieces set back from the main building. It now stands 43cm (17in.) high x 73.6cm (29in.) wide. Obviously Henshaw's are doing very well!

F.J. LEWIS & SONS ENGINEERS

When my friend Fred Lewis is not driving trains for a living, he is building them in 7mm! A great kit builder and weatherer of locos, to-date he has built me the Duchess No.46251 'City of Nottingham'. 9F No.92054, WD No.90057, Fairburn Tank No.42151 and 'weathered' and improved many more. It is also a joy to see Fred driving the steam specials along our famous stretch of coastline between Exeter and Newton Abbot. Long may he continue to tell me off for not cleaning my track and loco wheels enough!

Fred's factory stands 61cm (24in.) tall and 104cm (41in.) wide. On this occasion I have wiped off more of the black oil paint to show the brickwork a little cleaner than the others. Not all buildings would have the same degree of dirt.

CANAL WAREHOUSE & BASIN

To the left of F.J. Lewis & Sons, is the canal basin. The much begrimed goods depot straddling both railway sidings and canal is an adaptation from the previous layout but works quite well keeping low, allowing my painted backdrop above to show the gradual change from industrial townscape to the Pennine moorland.

A mirror is placed at the end of the canal to give the effect of continuation. I have done the same in the town between the Victoria Hotel and shoe shop.

The six storey canal warehouse with its 45 windows set in a stone pattern plasticard was great fun to build. I based it on the terminal warehouse in the Sheffield basin of the Sheffield and South Yorkshire navigation and squeezed it into this busy corner of the layout. The model is 68.5cm (27in.) high x 94cm (37in.) wide. The canal 'water' is a piece of 3mm (1/8in.) clear perspex. I drew the shape I needed on two large pieces of card, stuck them together then cut round the shape with a knife. A company in Newton Abbot make Perspex windows, I will never forget the look on the guy's face when I walked in with my 'canal shape' and told him what it was for! I painted the underside of the 'water' with a polluted looking colour mixed from brown, green and yellow ochre oil paint. Two coats to cover properly. Many of the canals in the 1950's and 60's were derelict so more imagination is required here.

BR meets Stanier as 2-6-4 tank types pass each other.

Canal basin and coal tower activity.

Entering the wharf, looking to the Pennines in the distance.

8F No.48523 and WD No. 90257 doublehead a coal train past the canal basin.

8F 48523, on a night coal train, passing canal basin.

THE
MARIAN
MILL

A t 96.5cm (38in.) high x 109.2cm (43in.) wide, above the small wharf building straddling the canal, is the Marian Mill, named after my mother who died in January 2014. My mother and father, 'Marian and Cliff', now sit opposite each other on the layout, memorials to my wonderful parents.

VICTORIA HOTEL

I may have been thinking of my old trainspotting haunt, Manchester Victoria, when I decided upon the Victoria Hotel. Made entirely of smooth card and painted in very dark greys to represent years of grime. This method saves money on Plasticard. Pieces of red paper stuck either side of the windows representing curtains. The walkway shop fronts were printed from photos I took of Widemarsh Street, Hereford, for their old fashioned look. My good friend David Mocatta, printed them to scale size. The two end walkways are painted in watercolour to give the impression of distance, looking through the building. 66cm (26in.) high x 111.7cm (44in.)wide.

Night time in Chadbury, the Victoria Hotel.

B1 61040 approaching the steel girder bridge.

THE STEEL GIRDER BRIDGE

The design of the bridge is based on the girder bridge known as Battledown Flyover on the ex Southern Railway at Worting Junction, where the Southampton and Bournemouth lines cross the West Country Waterloo line. Although this actual bridge is skewed due to the angle where the two lines meet (mine of course is parallel). A solid piece of wood for the track bed with the two sides made entirely of mount board. Gluing one piece between two to form a 'H' shape. It is amazing how strong this can be when all fixed together and painted. It slots into position across the doorway tightly making sure the track is perfectly in line left and right and level. It is 114.3cm (45in.) long and 19.6cm (7 ¾"in.) high in the centre. Wire to the track drops through and is connected by a joiner plug.

THE TOWN GARDENS

Below the Victoria Hotel lies the town gardens. A low relief area giving opportunity for people and road traffic. As per the canal, the boating lake is made from Perspex painted underneath in oils to achieve the water effect. Lawns interrupted with flowerbeds, a war memorial and some small trees all go to make up this recreation area. My cars and vans are mostly 'Vanguard' models at 1-43rd scale which is correct for 7mm 'O'gauge. The buses and some lorries however are out of size at 1-50th scale. I have difficulty in finding these vehicles at the correct scale. The gardens are 111.8cm (44in.) in length.

Night time in Chadbury gardens.

Courtship in the gardens.

"Hello Sarge, Constable Dixon here, I might have a spot of bother on my hands"

BOTTOMLEY'S MODEL SHOP

Well what can I say? If you cannot elevate yourself to shop owner on your own layout then it is a poor do! Not only does this building use up the remaining space allotted to the town but its triangular shape breaks up the 90 degree regularity of the other buildings. Possibly the oldest building on the layout with its half timbered corbelling and red tile roof makes for variety in shape and construction materials. Once again saving on plasticard, done very simply on mount board with strips of thin card glued down to represent the timbers. For the shop fronts I have created a 'box' in which to stick my photo prints of shop fronts, leaving the box shape open at the top to allow for the lighting. The Elizabethan style leaded windows are lines drawn in black biro on tracing paper to show through the plastic window. My store full of wonders measures 40.6cm (16in.) to rooftop x 53.3cm (21in.) wide.

Ex LMS Jubilee class 4-6-0 No.45717 'Dauntless' double heading Ex LNER B1 class 4-6-0 No.61040 'Roedeer' approach the bridge.

Main line activity passing the model shop.

PAULDENS (STORE)

I have named the store 'Pauldens' as this was one of Manchester's major stores at the top of Market St. in Piccadilly (formerly Rylands and later to become Debenhams). I must have walked past this store many times during the ten years in which I worked in advertising studios. I have only modelled the three sides visible. Proudly sitting on the roof is another inverted Christmas pudding bowl! The building measures 44.4cm (17.5in.) x 39.3cm (15.5in.) and 53.3cm (21in.) high plus centre pieces on top. The shop windows are from photos taken from 'Austins 'shops in Newton Abbot near where I live today. The building would be a typical 1920's/ 1930's design. Very smooth stonework with varying profiles created with various strips of mount board overlayed. The window frames I have drawn in position on tracing paper behind the clear plastic window apperture then placed the window divisions (thin strips of plastic or card) carefully using tweezers dipping them in glue and placing over the drawn lines. I have weathered the ground floor dirtier as this seemed to happen with traffic fumes and smoke etc.

9F meets a breakdown train.

BRIDGEWATER STREET

No Lancashire based layout of the 1950's would be complete without the ubiquitous terraced house. Row upon row of them spread throughout the townscape providing homes for factory and mill workers. Two up two down with a short yard at the back, was the basic accommodation for the working class. I have built my street as another section to the main layout, modelling it at a lower level with the road leading up to the main layout near the station.

I made a lightweight table 2.92m (9ft 7in.) wide by 66cm (26in.) across to accommodate the street, this was just wide enough to go through the doorway. I then added my canal, screwed to the table by three brackets making it 86.3cm (34in.) in total. This section can be easily pulled away to gain access to the rest of the layout for track cleaning purposes. The street seems like a separate community to the rest of the layout and comprises of, left to right, a pumping station for the canal, then the 'Rose of Lancaster' hotel, this was the name of my local pub in Chadderton. Opposite, is the pub car park, then a corrugated roofed Nissan hut built as a temporary building during the second world war. To the right of these are a series of terraced houses, those backed on to the canal showing the washing lines out to suggest a Monday morning! To the right of these is the 'Norton R Jensen ironworks' loading some of its produce on to a narrow boat. On the roadside above are typical advertising hoardings adding a bit of colour to the begrimed street below.

(The terraced houses and ironworks are mentioned in more detail in the book showing their construction).

Conversation piece by the canal.

Positioning Bridgewater Street up to the layout.

Bending plywood round the layout to form the retaining wall.

Retaining wall, half brick half stone.

Gluing stone edging to canal wall.

Looking down 'the cut'. Along with railways, another favourite playground.

"When I'm cleanin' winders"

"Hey Rita fancy going to a dance on Saturday"?

Brewery lorry replenishing the 'Rose of Lancaster Hotel'.

'Dirty old town'.

Looking left along the canal from the ironworks.

A chat over the fence after collecting his paper.

"Just finished. Now time for a pint in the Rose".

Another bag of nutty slack for no.8.

"Nevermind trainspotting, get that homework done"!

"Watch those pipes we can't afford another load to drop in the cut"!

PICKET FENCING

To make fencing to this extent is to test one's patience, so I recommend playing your favourite music with a break for tea and coffee at regular intervals.

This type of heavy duty fencing was common around railways and canals. Sometimes old railway sleepers were used around loco shed yards. I have used 3mm (8th in.) thick card cut with Stanley knife and steel rule to post widths of 6mm (¼ in.) wide and 54mm (2 & 1/8th) high. I first score the card with the knife then run down the score line with the sharp point of a bradall to give a rounded worn edge to the posts. Then I cut the pointed tops before cutting completely through the card to separate the posts. I then line up the posts with a thin piece of card between each one as a spacer (as you would when tiling a wall). I then glue them all together at the base using a length of 6mm (1/4 inch) quadrant wood moulding with PVA glue. This not only adds stability to your fence but the curved shape of the quadrant provides you with a bank effect on which to cover with grass. I have repeated this on the back of the fence to give a wider base when gluing it down on the layout. Another strip of card glued near the top will complete the job. To add realism I have missed out the odd post and broken one or two. (These gaps, as I

remember, allowed us as young trainspotters to get through and take our chances in the engine shed.)

To finish off I have painted the fence very dark brown, almost black as they were covered in tar to prevent them rotting.

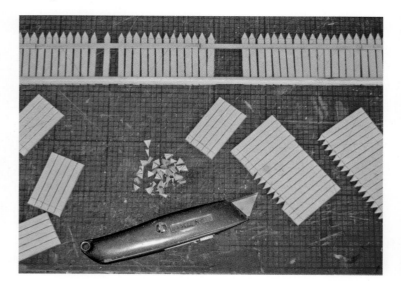

LOCOMOTIVE SHED

The loco shed has only 2 roads as any more would eat up too much space. I have used a fairly rough grade stone plasticard for the walls and office. It is 81.2cm (32in.) long including the office at the rear, and 25.3cm (10in.) wide. The roof venting is made from strips of mount board slotted at intervals into wall sections keeping it parallel. This roof vented section took me almost as long as the rest of the entire shed! The windows are metal moulded similar to those used for the 'Howells engineering' building (opposite page). Standing outside the shed is my ex LMS 4-6-0 Black 5 no. 45348 built by a good friend from a Javelin kit designed by Dave Andrews. He also built my 0-6-0 class 3F 'Jinty'no. 47318 from a Jim McGowan 'Connoisseur'kit. I have had all my loco's numbered after engines I actually saw in my trainspotting days.

"What's going on here lads, can your parents afford the fine for trespassing ?"

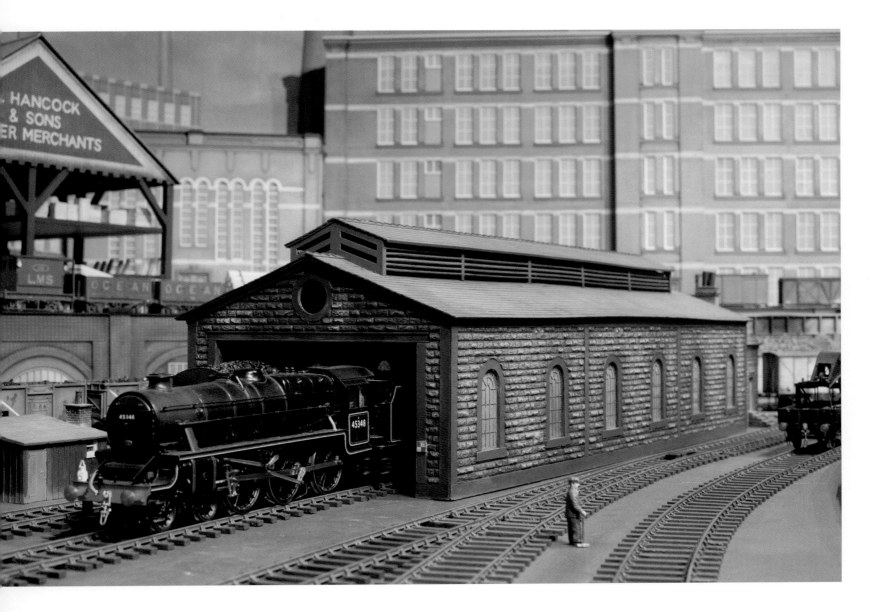

Chadbury motive power depot yard.

A full house - it must be Sunday!

Any colour as long as it's black!

Kit built Ex LMS Fairburn 2-6-4T. No.42115 sits back to back with 'ready to run' B.R. 2-6-4T. No.80046.

Week-end favourite playground.

Austin Somerset meets B.R. parcels van.

WATER TOWER & COALING STAGE

This tower was based on various ex LMS coal and water plants. Chester and Patricroft (Manchester) in particular, influenced this structure. Making the water tank I used a door surround moulding then copied the curved edge with a piece of half-round stripwood to give me a symmetrical 'tank' shape. Then I cut the timber carefully using a mitre block. The 'water' itself is the smooth side of hardboard painted dark grey with various coats of gloss varnish.

The wagon ramp running through the tower is quite narrow 63mm (2.5in.) wide x 147.3cm (58in.) long to get the loco close enough for tender filling. I have chopped the sleeper ends off to fit.

8F 48523 under the coaler as A3 'Dick Turpin' waits in the yard.

9F 2-10-0 No. 92054 being
'fed and watered'

Another typical combination
of loco's in late '50's
Lancashire as WD 90257
passes Jubilee 'Dauntless'

CHADBURY STATION

This is a typical ex Lancashire & Yorkshire wood boarded station, in my case made entirely from mountboard, with card strips again overlaid for the roof tiles. The use of mini-posters and timetable boards help to break up the timberwork. The rail side of the station is cut in a way to sit over the platform. The station dimensions are 34.2cm (13.5in.) long x 140mm (5.5in.) deep x 107mm (4.25in.) high from roadside to base of roof.

Station Road runs around the back of Bridgewater Street parallel to the goods line from the station to the rear of the loco shed. Not having the luxury of fiddle yards this line provides accommodation for another train.

"They'll never get rid of steam trains, mark my words"

Ex Midland Rly. 0-4-4T. No.58074 waits in the station with a local train.

Looking past the B.R. workers coach up Station Road.

Stanier Black 5 No.45348 with B1 leaves, as Ex Midland Rly. Johnson 0-4-4 Tank approaches the station.

A wide shot of Chadbury station showing sky and townscape backdrop, plus municipal museum building behind.

Ex LNER A3 class No.60080 'Dick Turpin' approaches the station while the ex Midland Rly. tank coals up.

Ex war department loco No.90257 is about to leave Station Rd. goods siding.

SIGNAL BOX & FOOTBRIDGE

These are the only buildings on the layout that I cannot lay claim to have made, although I did have to make a new roof with my own tiling as the plastic roof was not very convincing. I bought it as a kit and then situated it onto a gantry adapted from various girder strips and a footbridge kit. The footbridge itself is actually two footbridge kits adapted to fit over three platforms.

The two tank loco's wait patiently for work while the 'Pug' on the timber line passes above.

TRACKWORK WIRING & SOUND

Each piece of individual track is connected by a pair of dropper wires to a dual busbar underneath the layout in addition to using rail joiners. The section comprising the engine shed and associated sidings is able to be switched out of circuit so that locomotives not yet fitted with decoders can be placed on the isolated track. Some turnouts are fitted with internal microswitches to change the polarity of the frog prior to them being wired through an external slide switch, which also performs the required mechanical linkage to change direction. Others will be left with just the internal microswitch connected and changed over by hand, especially in the sidings.

Two entirely separate end to end tracks are powered via Heathcote Electronics circuits with detectors fitted between the rails at each end so that trains are reversed after a pre-determined delay. As soon as power is supplied on the 'Cliff' cotton mill line an 'idle steam' sound is heard which changes to a 'shunting' sound while moves are taking place; the same sounds are then repeated at the other end of the line.

A second DC operated locomotive (the L&Y Pug) and wagons operate along what is known as 'the timber line' in the same way as the previous line only longer between 'Hancocks timber' and behind the town of Chadbury.

I intend to add 'loco shed and depot' sounds in line with the remaining locomotives being installed with decoders. Sounds have been edited using 'Audacity', a downloadable program on the web. All of the sounds are delivered via conveniently located modules connected to small amplifiers and loudspeakers adjacent to the relevant parts of the layout.

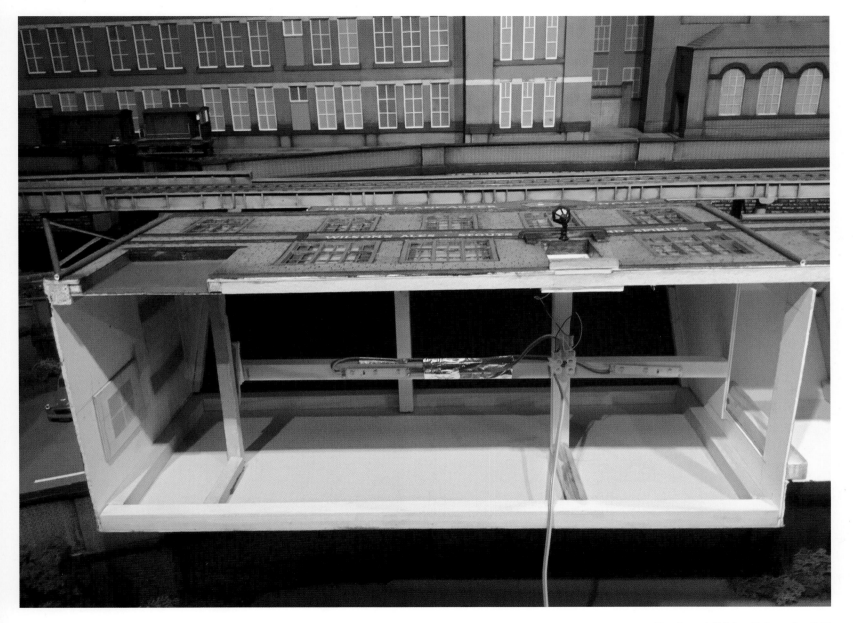

LIGHTING OF BUILDINGS

Lighting for the buildings is achieved by different methods using light emitting diodes, grain of wheat bulbs and a fluorescent strip! The latter method is used for the 'Cliff' cotton mill depicting prototypical flooding of light around the looms. For safety reasons this is powered through a residual current device.

Light emitting diodes are attached in strips of three inside various buildings with the interconnected wiring taped to the structure. Some of the LED's are placed above or below windows facing backwards and reflecting off a white backing sheet. Other sets of three LED's face downwards from various levels of the buildings. White lighting prevails but some older buildings such as the L&Y warehouse, the canal warehouse and 'Howells Engineering' have yellow LED's fitted.

Shop lighting is fitted above the display windows in order to show off their wares to better effect. All of the tall buildings are fitted with a single strip of LED's to either illuminate the clock faces or highlight the attic spaces. The 'Victoria Hotel' is fitted with grain of wheat bulbs such that not all of the individual rooms are illuminated although the ground level shop fronts are fully lit. The 'Museum' is also fitted with grain of wheat bulbs.

In the future, platform lights for the station, lighting the loco shed area and road lights will be added along with possibly Belisha beacons and traffic lights etc.

There is a 12volt 10 amp power supply fed to the lighting via a ring main and terminal blocks using thick cable to prevent volts drop at remote locations from the source.

8F No. 48523 with a night freight passes the old canal wharf building.

I have included this painting I did of the Staple Inn, Holborn, London as an example of how I wanted the night time lighting effect.

'Dick Turpin' enters Chadbury while 'Roedeer' waits to leave.

WEATHERING

As a lifelong painter in oils my own brand of weathering materials have always been at hand. There is no better medium to my mind than oils, not only for the perfect blending and feathering achieved, but for the length of time allowed to get it right.

For the brick and stonework effect I have always used Slaters plasticard covering it in black oil paint I then get a cloth and wipe off the necessary amount leaving the paint in the crevices exposing the brick and stone bond clearly. In the case of extremely dirty buildings leave more of the paint on. Chimney tops etc. can be solid black. Loco sheds and surrounding buildings and walls will also need to be very dirty. When the oil paint is dry you can add more in the form of streaking and staining using a dry brush and dragging down other colours. For instance the base of walls and around drainpipes can be greenish mouldy colours. Building roofs can be stained down across the tiles such as white marks from the lead around chimneys. Extra dirt can be added later, wiping off any excess as you go. A list of useful oil paint colours would be:

French Ultramarine and Burnt Umber - these two colours mixed together will make black. I do not use black oil paint as it takes far too long to dry.

Titanium White - is a pure white and mixed in varying degrees with the above will give you greys for roof tiles, roads, pavements, railway station platforms etc.

Olive Green, Yellow Ochre and Burnt Sienna - these are what I call 'earth' colours, and mixed together with white can be used for grassy areas, pathways or even over track work.

I built 20 coal wagon's from Parkside Dundas kits then weathered them in oil paint. Applying the 'black' (mixture of blue and brown) then with a cloth and a dry brush took off most of the paint leaving it the corners where the dirt would collect. Then using a small brush, dotted in the rust spots using a reddish brown (burnt sienna)

Again with a dry brush, preferably a flat brush cut short, I can stipple the paint to give a textured effect on the ground. A small decorating brush could be used for larger areas.

Ballasting track work can be expensive, time consuming and prevents you ultimately from taking up the track and re-laying. A good substitute (as seen on the layout) is a mixture of brown, blue and white oil paint brushed over the track forming a grey/brown colour. Then the rail itself carefully in a rusty colour mixed from Burnt Sienna and white. Steadying your hand with a ruler while dragging a small brush along the rail then carefully wiping the top of the rail with a clean rag.

RECYCLING

In our 'green' age of 'saving the planet' even a model railway can play a small part in recycled materials. The tops of the Marian Mill and the Pauldens Store are inverted small Christmas Pudding bowls. On the four corners of the Cliff Mill tower top you will find shampoo bottle tops. A birthday cake candle holder sits at the very top of Howells Engineering. When painted grey they can all appear realistic. Different card thicknesses for different jobs can start with cornflake boxes and go up to heavy duty card found in product packaging. Lolly pop sticks and wooden skewers are fine for boarding and telegraph poles. It is always worth asking if you can buy the thick card or 2mm MDF that picture framers use to back their pictures. Also ask for unwanted mount board. They tend to throw away the centres of picture mounts they have cut, but tell them what you want it for or they will think you are setting up in competition!

FOOTNOTE

Building this model railway has been and will continue to be a great joy. It has been a journey through sheets of mount board, MDF, plasticard, pots of glue and tubes of paint. I am sure like all creative work it will have its critics. I will just have to hope that the most ardent of them will show some leniency in their judgement, particularly of my spacial cheating throughout the layout. As we know 'O' gauge eats up space very quickly, hence the art of fitting a quart into a pint pot is necessary. Let us face it, we are inside a double garage after all and those white metal figures sat patiently waiting for a train they will never catch because they are glued to the seat - are not real!

There will always be more work needed; on studying the track plan you will see the outside track is isolated from the rest of the trackwork, so two more points required.

Telegraph poles, ballasting, more signalling needed. I have in mind to add another street section at right angles to Bridgewater Street. Brewery Street, not surprisingly starting at the brewery would run downhill to meet the canal. A row of stone cottages would run down the hill opposite the brewery complex. But not yet - my next project is back to the easel for my second art book, this time with Pen & Sword.

As a painter of transport subjects for over forty years creating this model has been a welcome diversion from the two to the three dimension. Capturing the same subjects I love in a differing way.

I can only now hope that I might have captured the inspiration of the 'would be' modeller to have a go at creating their 'other world'.

Master of all he surveys.

"Now you've finished the book
get me out of here"